# Life Skills

# Cooking a Meal

by Emma Huddleston

# www.focusreaders.com

Focus Readers is distributed by North Star Editions:
sales@northstareditions.com | 888-417-0195

Produced for Focus Readers by Red Line Editorial.

Photographs ©: iStockphoto, cover, 1, 4, 7, 8, 11, 12, 15 (measuring cups), 16, 19; Shutterstock Images, 15 (measuring spoons), 21

**Library of Congress Cataloging-in-Publication Data**
Names: Huddleston, Emma, author.
Title: Cooking a meal / Emma Huddleston.
Description: Lake Elmo : Focus Readers, 2021. | Series: Life skills |
   Includes index. | Audience: Grades 2–3
Identifiers: LCCN 2019057381 (print) | LCCN 2019057382 (ebook) | ISBN
   9781644933435 (hardcover) | ISBN 9781644934197 (paperback) | ISBN
   9781644935712 (pdf) | ISBN 9781644934951 (ebook)
Subjects: LCSH: Cooking--Juvenile literature. | Children--Life skills
   guides--Juvenile literature.
Classification: LCC TX652.5 .H83 2021  (print) | LCC TX652.5  (ebook) | DDC
   641.5--dc23
LC record available at https://lccn.loc.gov/2019057381
LC ebook record available at https://lccn.loc.gov/2019057382

Printed in the United States of America
Mankato, MN
082020

## About the Author

Emma Huddleston lives in the Twin Cities with her husband. They cook at least two meals together each week. Emma enjoys writing children's books and reading.

# Table of Contents

# Chapter 1

# Why Cooking Matters

People eat food every day.

Food gives people energy.

The **nutrients** in food help

people stay healthy.

Some foods are not ready to eat right away. They need to be **prepared**. Cooking is when people get food ready for eating. Cooking food often means heating it.

**Fun Fact**

People can save money by cooking. It costs less than eating out.

# Chapter 2

# Gathering Ingredients

People make meals with **ingredients**. These foods can be wet or dry. Water and oil are wet ingredients. Flour and sugar are dry.

People wash their hands before cooking. Then they prepare the ingredients. For example, they may cut vegetables. They may set butter out to soften. Or they may rip leaves off **herbs**.

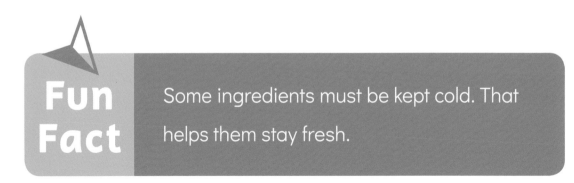

**Fun Fact**

Some ingredients must be kept cold. That helps them stay fresh.

2 stick mar...
(2C) 2 egg beaten
1 t orange ju...
(4T) 3 T vanilla (2t)
all dry ingredients - add butter ...
...ke - 1/2 t - far apart on
...num foil - cool thoroughly
...re - cannot use foil more than once
(over)
350° - 8-11 min ... crust
...snap crust is yu...

...gg yolks lightly. Add cond. milk, (sweetened) b...
...gain. Add lime juice + beat until
...mooth. Pour into pie shell. Bake 350° - 5

...marga...
...pped mil...
...colate bits

...heat oven to 400° : Rinse chicken and
pat dry. Squeeze juice of orange
quarters over chicken (inside + out). ...
onion + orange pieces over (inside) b...
Sprinkle salt + pepper + rosemary. Pla...
chicken in roasting pan + pour water
pan. Roast 20 min. Reduce heat t...
...and roast 1 hr. * If using ...
...approx. 40 min...

# Chapter 3

# Following a Recipe

A **recipe** tells how to make a meal. It has a list of ingredients. It also tells how much of each ingredient is needed.

People **measure** out the ingredients. They use measuring cups and spoons. Then they follow the steps of the recipe.

Safety is important when cooking. People may need to use an oven or stove. They may need to use knives. An adult should be around to help.

# Measuring Cups
# and Spoons

1 cup

½ cup

⅓ cup

¼ cup

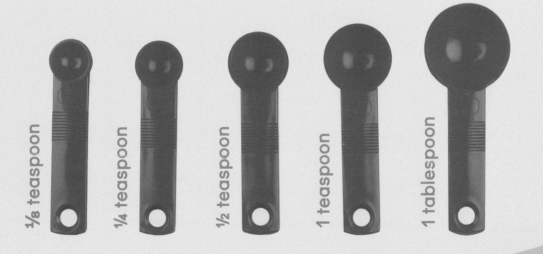

⅛ teaspoon

¼ teaspoon

½ teaspoon

1 teaspoon

1 tablespoon

# Chapter 4

# Mealtime

The final step is to put everything together. People might mix ingredients in a bowl. Or they might **bake** ingredients in a pan.

Cooking takes time and work. But the result is a good meal. Many people enjoy sharing meals with others. They serve food to show they care.

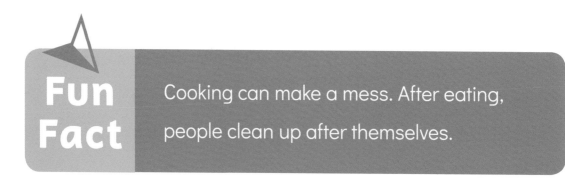

**Fun Fact** Cooking can make a mess. After eating, people clean up after themselves.

# Sandwich Pinwheels

## Ingredients

- 3 tablespoons (45 mL) of mayonnaise
- 1 tablespoon (15 mL) of mustard
- 1 large tortilla
- 1 large lettuce leaf
- 2 slices of cheese
- 2 slices of ham (optional)

## Steps

1. Mix the mayonnaise and mustard.
2. Lay the tortilla flat. Spread the sauce on the tortilla.
3. Place the lettuce, cheese, and ham on the tortilla.
4. Roll the tortilla tightly.
5. Cut the roll into eight pieces. Ask an adult for help.

# FOCUS ON
# Cooking a Meal

*Write your answers on a separate piece of paper.*

1. Write a sentence that tells the main idea of Chapter 1.

2. Cooking a meal includes gathering ingredients and following a recipe. Which step do you think is most important? Why?

3. What does a recipe include?
    A. the amount of each ingredient needed
    B. how to clean up after cooking
    C. a list of nutrients in each food

4. What might happen if someone doubles the amounts of the ingredients?
    A. The person might make twice as much food.
    B. The meal might not taste as good.
    C. The meal might cook faster than expected.

*Answer key on page 24.*

# Glossary

**bake**
To heat in the oven.

**herbs**
Plants that are used to make food taste a certain way.

**ingredients**
Foods that are mixed together to make a meal.

**measure**
To find the amount of something.

**nutrients**
Things that people, animals, and plants need to stay healthy.

**prepared**
Made ready to be used.

**recipe**
A list of ingredients and steps needed to make a meal.

# To Learn More

## BOOKS

Kuskowski, Alex. *Super Simple Classic Cookies: Easy Cookie Recipes for Kids!* Minneapolis: Abdo Publishing, 2016.

Ventura, Marne. *Bacon Artist: Savory Bacon Recipes.* North Mankato, MN: Capstone Press, 2017.

## NOTE TO EDUCATORS

Visit **www.focusreaders.com** to find lesson plans, activities, links, and other resources related to this title.

# Index

**Answer Key: 1.** Answers will vary; **2.** Answers will vary; **3.** A; **4.** A